Bisbee, Arizona
Then and Now

Boyd Nicholl

Edited by Janice Coggin

Cowboy Miner
PRODUCTIONS

Bisbee, Arizona, Then and Now
Copyright © 2003 Cowboy Miner Productions
Modern photographs copyright © 2003 Boyd Nicholl

Publisher:
   Cowboy Miner Productions
   P.O. Box 9674
   Phoenix, AZ 85068
   Phone: (602) 569-6063
   www.CowboyMiner.com

Publisher's Cataloging-in-Publication Data
Nicholl, Boyd, 1945—
Bisbee, Arizona, Then and Now / Boyd Nicholl, photographer.
   p. cm. Illustrated.
   ISBN: 1-931725-10-1
1. Western History (U.S.) 2. Historic Photos—Western. 3. History—Bisbee, Arizona.
4. Architecture—Bisbee, Arizona
   I. Title
Library of Congress Control Number: 2003096940

Design & Typesetting: SageBrush Publications, Tempe, Arizona
Cover Design: ATG Productions, Phoenix, Arizona
Printing: Bang Printing, Brainerd, Minnesota
Cover Photo: Panorama of 1907 Bisbee.

Historical photos compliments of Bisbee Mining & Historical Museum.

Printed and bound in the United States of America

To those who lived in Bisbee "then" and those who live there now

Table of Contents

Foreword. 6

Then and Now. 7

Introduction—Bisbee, Arizona 9

A note on the photographs. 11

Castle Rock, c. 1882 12

Looking west from Castle Rock, c. 1892. 14

Overlooking downtown, c. 1893. 16

Copper Queen Smelter, c. 1898 18

Phelps Dodge Mercantile in 1902 20

Copper Queen library, c. 1902 22

The north side of Main Street looking west, c. 1903 . . 24

The Bank of Bisbee, c. 1903 26

Interior of the Bank of Bisbee, c. 1903 28

Looking North up Brewery Gulch, c. 1904 30

Looking northeast over downtown, c. 1906 32

Looking west from Chihuahua Hill, c. 1906 34

Upper Brewery Gulch, c. 1907 36

Copper Queen Hotel, c. 1907 38

Presbyterian Church, c. 1902 40

Looking east down Main Street, c. 1908. 42

Erie Street in Lowell, c. 1910 44

Bisbee Railroad Station, c. 1910 46

YMCA, c. 1914. 48

Bisbee High School, c. 1913 50

Phelps Dodge Copper Queen Office, c. 1912 52

Copper Queen Mine, c. 1917 54

Cougdon Boulevard in Warren, c. 1917 56

Interior of the St. Elmo, c. 1919 58

City Park, c. 1917 60

Fire Station, c. 1917 62

Brewery Gulch looking down the canyon, c. 1920. . 64

Castle Rock, c. 1932 66

Main Street and Chihuahua Hill, c. 1938 68

The Top Café, c. 1947 70

Pythian Castle, c. 1957 72

St. Patrick's Church, c. 1957 74

Main Street, c. 1957 76

Foreword

*E*nter Bisbee and turn back the clock.

Situated in southeastern Arizona, Bisbee gained prominence as a mining center in the late nineteenth century. Today's Bisbee preserves this atmosphere, set in the matrix of the West's once extensive copper kingdom. The stately turn-of-the-century buildings of the historic downtown emanate the wealth generated by the city's copper mines founded to answer the call of the Age of Electricity.

With a history deserving of National Landmark status, it's only fitting that Bisbee's past be captured in a visual accounting of its architectural landscape.

Boyd Nicholl has been on the staff of the Bisbee Mining & Historical Museum for more than a decade. I know, firsthand, his love of and dedication to bringing Bisbee's history out of the Museum's archives and to the general public. Combined with his years of researching Bisbee history, Boyd is also a professional photographer, completing his AA, Photography, from Rochester Institute of Technology and BFA, Photography, from the University of Arizona. In *Bisbee, Arizona, Then and Now*, Mr. Nicholl combines his talents in providing an annotated tour through the contours of Bisbee's architectural history, then and now.

Carrie Gustavson, Director
Bisbee Mining & Historical Museum

Then and Now

The visual record of a city past and present, these pages revisit Bisbee, Arizona, as nineteenth century boomtown and as twenty-first century community. Juxtaposing historic photos with their modern counterpart, each turn of the page reveals its own story.

Standing in the footprints of the original photographers, Boyd Nicholl has captured the modern view of life in Bisbee, even taking care to photograph the scene in weather conditions similar to the historic original.

What strikes the viewer in turning these pages is not simply the changes Bisbee has experienced. Surprising, too, is how little Bisbee has changed. More than other modern cities, Bisbee has retained—and celebrates—a rich heritage. Many historic buildings dominate the same corners of town upon which they were originally constructed.

Whether you choose to experience these photos from your armchair or Bisbee's historic streets, savor this unforgettable journey of past and present, historic and modern, then and now.

Introduction—Bisbee, Arizona

*M*y writer friends say I cannot write that Bisbee is nestled in the Mule Mountains, but it is a fact! Maybe not nestled, as that is very anthropomorphic in tone; nonetheless, our small city is definitely in the canyons of these southeastern Arizona mountains. With a mean altitude of 5,500 feet above sea level, Bisbee is an island in the surrounding deserts. Oak and juniper dot the hillsides, and when the summer monsoons come, the clouds dance over the hilltops. The canyon's colors are rust reds and limestone grays with soft sea greens of trees and bushes—a gentle palate, pleasant to the eyes. Living at this altitude in the desert is wonderful. A climate with all four seasons, summer not too hot and winter with just enough snow to be interesting, makes for a fine spot.

Bisbee has a remarkable history for such a small town. Far from any major city, it was once the powerhouse of Arizona. Copper was what made Bisbee great—billions of tons of the red metal were wrested from these mountains to fuel the electrical age. Electricity was just coming on line when high-grade copper ore was discovered here.

A platoon of U.S. Army troops, under the command of Lt. Anthony Rucker, patrolling for signs of hostile Apaches stopped here to rest and water their mounts early in 1877. At several places in the canyon, they noticed copper stain and found chunks of native copper. In the early days of the West, it was not unusual for soldiers to do a little prospecting on the side, and this led Rucker and his scout Jack Dunn to file the first claims in the Mule Mountains that same year.

Impressed with the possibilities of a rich ore find, Rucker and Dunn grubstaked an itinerant prospector named George Warren to return to the Mules and file more claims for them. Now Ol' George, after a spell of boozing, did show up in Mule Gulch and did proceed to file new mining claims but neglected to include Rucker and Dunn on any of them. One of the claims George filed would later become the successful Copper Queen Mine. In the following year, more than two hundred claims were filed in the Mule Mountains, and the population of Bisbee in the winter of '78 swelled to eleven!

Copper mining takes big capital; it was not until 1880 that Ed Reilly, a mining entrepreneur, went to San Francisco with his new option on the Copper Queen mine and found backing from the Bisbee and Williams Development Company. Dewitt Bisbee put up $80,000, a fortune in that day, to get the Queen underway. Mr. Williams's sons were hired, and in short order the Copper Queen was in production, complete with its own smelter.

The early residents, when applying for their first Post Office, decided to name the town after Dewitt, and Bisbee was on the map. The ore was tremendously high-grade and profits soared from the get-go. Quickly the town began to grow: saloons, grocery stores, and barber shops were built on the one piece of flat ground Mule Gulch had to offer—the canyon bottom. So when looking at the images of Main Street, viewers will find it exactly in the same place 123 years later.

In 1881, James Douglas, in the employ of several speculators including the then Phelps and Dodge Mercantile Company, came to Bisbee looking for mining property. He liked what he saw in the Atlanta Claim, directly above the Queen, and advised Phelps and Dodge to take an option on the Atlanta. Legal matters took some time, and the first two years of exploration yielded no worthwhile ore. It was not until 1885 that Phelps Dodge made a serious strike. Both the Copper Queen and P.D. hit the John Smith Stope that year. Bisbee's future as a major mining center was assured. Under the direction of James Douglas, the two companies merged into the Copper Queen Consolidated Mining Company and became in time one of the world's largest mining outfits.

Starting in the late 1890s, other mining men built great mining operations here. From Michigan came the Hoatson brothers, helping to create the Calumet and Arizona Mining Company. At its peak, the company operated seven very successful mines in the Southwest. The C. and A. founded the community of Warren—Arizona's first planned city, built an interurban railway, and prospered for many years.

Locals like Lemual Shattuck and Joseph Muheim also got into the game, building great fortunes from the mineral resources found in Bisbee's red hills.

The city of Bisbee grew right along with the mining and became an "Urban Outpost on the Frontier." Phelps Dodge brought a rail line into town; one could buy a fancy suit of clothes, get fresh oysters, or ride to Chicago for the opera. Due to the many fires in the early days, ordinances were passed requiring commercial buildings to be made of brick, the result being the lovely early-twentieth-century town we have today. Bisbee is often referred to as unique, and that it is, for sure. One of its most unique aspects is that, for some unknown reason, the buildings have not been remodeled but left in their original form. Walking down Main Street or Brewery Gulch today is visually much as it was more than a hundred years ago.

A note on the photographs

The "then" photographs are all from the collection of the Bisbee Mining & Historical Museum. The Museum holds some 25,000 images of Bisbee from all its different phases. The old town has attracted photographers, both professional and amateur, from its earliest days. The "now" pictures try to duplicate as much as possible the earlier images, but because of physical changes in the town and in photography itself, it is not possible to get exactly the same feel or viewpoint. I hope you enjoy this comparative view of Bisbee. It is a city I have come to truly love.

Boyd Nicholl

Castle Rock, c. 1882

$\mathcal{T}$he first ore was discovered by Lt. Anthony Rucker and Jack Dunn at the base of Castle Rock. George Warren's cabin is located at the front center of the photo on the left. George Warren was one of the first prospectors in the Mule Mountains and the man for whom the mining district was later named.

Looking west from Castle Rock, c. 1892

*T*he cabin in the foreground, in the historical photo, was used for a short time as one of Bisbee's first schools. The area was called Quality Hill for the past hundred years and featured homes of several executives of the mining companies. A climb up the stairs in the modern picture leads to a pleasant walk and a view of the architecture of the stately homes lining the old streets.

Overlooking downtown, c. 1893

*I*n 1893, houses sheltering the miners huddled around the Glory Hole, on the left, and Bisbee's first successful mining operations, center. The Copper Queen smelter was in full production,

down the canyon. The mountain Sacramento Hill, in the background of the 1893 picture, disappeared into the Sacramento open pit mine beginning in 1917. In the modern photo, business buildings, hotels, and schools have replaced many of the homes.

Copper Queen Smelter, c. 1898

*T*he photo on the left was taken just before the smelter was moved to Douglas, Arizona. At this time, five furnaces were in use and the copper flowed like a river from Bisbee. Enough ore was produced to make Bisbee a "Bonanza Camp"—7.7 billion pounds of copper, 100 million ounces of silver and 2.7 million ounces of gold. The modern photo shows a few remnants of the busy operations.

Phelps Dodge Mercantile in 1902

Phelps Dodge Mercantile, at one point, had seven stores in the area. The smaller building to the left was the "new" furniture department. Miners were able to "charge" their purchases and have them subtracted from their wages. In later years, it was possible to clothe the family, outfit

the kitchen, furnish the home, and buy the groceries without leaving the building. Large purchases could be bought on time, with no interest and a certain amount subtracted from the wages each payday.

Copper Queen library, c. 1902

$\mathcal{O}$n Main Street, the library was a gift to the city from the Phelps Dodge Mining Company and continued to be run by the company until the 1960s. The post office is located on the first floor, below the library in the modern photo. Due to the steep hills, Bisbee offers no home mail delivery, so the post office remains a good place to meet neighbors.

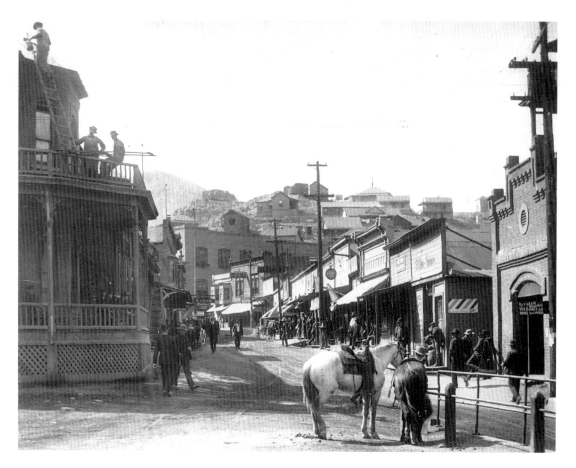

The north side of Main Street looking west, c. 1903

*T*he building on the right edge of the old photo was the Fire Station with St. Elmo's Saloon next door. The Elmo, one of Arizona's longest operating saloons, is still enjoyed by patrons today. Note the painters on the roof of the library across the street. The St. Elmo's Saloon was moved to Brewery Gulch sometime between 1906 and 1909.

The Bank of Bisbee, c. 1903

*T*he Bank of Bisbee, built by the "Main Street Crowd" and Phelps Dodge executives, was the first bank in the area. The original building was expanded after 1908 but maintained the original details. The house in the background (left photo) is the home of the Williams-Douglas family. The horsepower in today's trucks has replaced the burro power of old Bisbee.

Interior of the Bank of Bisbee, c. 1903

*N*ote the table from the original bank is still in use, but the old-fashioned grillwork and bulb lights are gone today. The marble kick plate on the floor is still present, but the spittoons have vanished.

Looking North up Brewery Gulch, c. 1904

Brewery Gulch, home to Bisbee's varied immigrant population, was a roaring success by 1904.
A Serbian, Mr. Medigavich, housed his grocery and the Moose Hall in the fine two-story building.

More recently, both buildings on the left were Medigavich properties. Today the street is definitely quieter! The Muheim Building (the Brewery) was built to the right after this photo was made in 1904.

Looking northeast over downtown, c. 1906

*T*he scene at left shows the downtown area two years before the great 1908 fire that destroyed most of the foreground buildings. Notice that at this time, the B had not been added to Chihuahua Hill. One of Bisbee's unique aspects is that the modern view shows the post-1908 structures still intact.

Looking west from Chihuahua Hill, c. 1906

From this pair of images, viewers can see how remarkably Bisbee has been preserved. Most of the major structures are still in place. To locate the area from which the photo was taken, use the tower of the Pythian Castle in the foreground as a guide. Note the increase in vegetation.

Upper Brewery Gulch, c. 1907

*T*his part of Bisbee was the "red light" district. The steps on the right led to "cribs" used by the "ladies of the night." Prostitution was outlawed in Bisbee not long after this photograph. Notice the "lady," at left, hiding her face behind her hands? The other woman was caught in the middle of the street. Several houses, now gone, line the hill behind the road. Today's view is a rather lonely quiet area.

Copper Queen Hotel, c. 1907

The Copper Queen Hotel, built by Phelps Dodge, is a fine Hailer Romanesque design. Today it is a fun lodging place reputed to have several ghosts. The bar, restaurant, and meeting rooms have made this edifice a popular meeting place over the years.

Presbyterian Church,
c. 1902

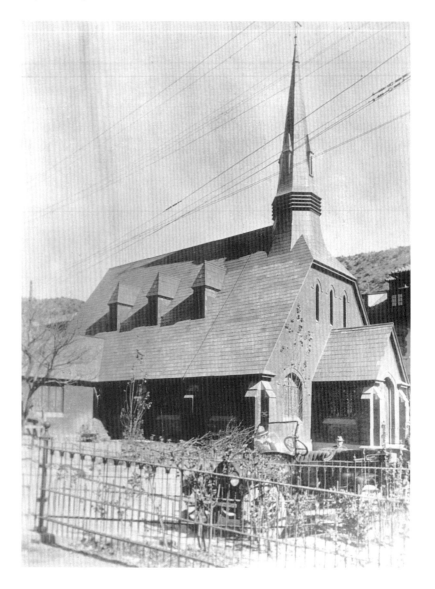

*L*ocated to the west of the Copper Queen Hotel, the Presbyterian Church was erected in 1902. The designers, Parrich and Schroeder, built it as a copy of the Dutch Reformed Church.

Looking east down Main Street, c. 1908

*O*n a rainy day ninety-five years later, Main Street is wonderfully much the same. The largest change is the "new mercantile" located at the end of the street. The old mercantile burned in 1938, and Del Webb of Sun City fame built the "new merc" we see today.

Erie Street in Lowell, c. 1910

$\mathcal{L}$owell now has pretty much been swallowed by the Lavender Pit, but in its day, it was a thriving community fondly remembered by Bisbee old timers. At one time, Lowell's main street hosted the Balich Bakery, the White House Cafe, a movie theater, Water's clothing store, a drugstore, the Pay and Tote Grocery, Ortega's shoes, the Brophy Garage, Whiteheads' Furniture, The Waiting Room Saloon, and Garcia's Tortillas, to name a few!

Bisbee Railroad Station, c. 1910

In the early days, the train pulled right into town, bringing passengers, goods, and mining equipment. Train passengers were said to "ride the cushions" into town, a definite luxury over buggies and carts. A multitude of homes, many now only a memory, crowded the hill in the old photograph. Now the station is gone, torn down in the early fifties, and automobiles have replaced the "cushions."

YMCA, c. 1914

*T*his elegant brick building housed the YMCA. In later years, a swimming pool was built in the basement of the building. Today the restored building is the "Gym Club" apartments.

In the 1914 photo, note the fitted rock wall work so prevalent in Bisbee. Walls were built so that rainwater, rushing down the hills could drain through the walls without washing yards and roads into the gulch. Water would collect behind solid walls built without drainpipes and eventually bulge and destroy the wall.

Bisbee High School, c. 1913

$\mathcal{T}$he old high school built on Clawson Avenue, later known as "High School Hill," now houses several county offices. The building is listed in Ripley's "Believe It or Not" due to its three stories that each boast a street-level entrance. Students had their choice of climbing stairs inside the building or going outside to climb the hill to the next story entrance. The gym was located on the top floor. According to rumor, it was placed there to keep students physically fit on their way to gym class!

Phelps Dodge Copper Queen Office, c. 1912

*O*n payday the miners are lined up in front of the company headquarters to collect their wages. Now the Bisbee Mining and Historical Museum, dedicated to the story of Bisbee and its fantastic mining heritage, resides within. The museum also houses an excellent library for those interested in the past history of the district.

Copper Queen Mine, c. 1917

*M*iners wait outside the change house by the haulage entrance to the Copper Queen. The variety of hats, a necessity in that era, is always interesting. Once one of Bisbee's richest mines, it is today the setting for the Copper Queen Mine Tour. Visitors are dressed for safety in hard hats, slickers, lamps, and belts. Retired miners explain the workings of the underground mine as they guide the tours.

Cougdon Boulevard in Warren, c. 1917

$\mathcal{F}$acing due east down one of Warren's main streets, the homes have changed very little. Warren, designed as one of Arizona's first planned communities, met the need for more beautiful housing and open vistas. Several streets were named after the directors of the Calumet and Arizona Mining Company, one of the large mining companies in the district.

Interior of the St. Elmo, c. 1919

*I*n 1919, Arizona was dry, and this long-established saloon was converted to an ice cream parlor. Now the saloon is back. Located in Brewery Gulch, the famed St. Elmo is worth a visit to see the hundreds of artifacts that decorate its old walls. Any book on Bisbee has at least one story set in or around the old bar. St. Elmo was originally built on Main Street in 1902.

City Park, c. 1917

*C*ity Park, once the town cemetery, was constructed in 1915. The gathering shown at left is for Loyalty Sunday arranged by the Loyalty League. The League stood for patriotism as America entered into the First World War. Note the wide variety of hats on both men and women. Not only the style of the day, wearing hats also protected residents from the blazing Arizona sun. Bodies from the cemetery were transferred to Evergreen Cemetery when the park was constructed.

Fire Station, c. 1917

*A*nother scene in Bisbee frozen in time, the fire station stands virtually unchanged. Fires were a constant danger to homes built of wood. Coal oil and wood stoves formed a lethal combination. The new image pictures Bisbee's 1941 fire engine, especially built to navigate the narrow hillside streets. The fire station also hosts modern engines.

Brewery Gulch looking down the canyon, c. 1920

*I*n this grouping, you can see how many of the homes have been lost over the years. Many were claimed by fires, and some were just torn down for the materials. Stairs are often the only way to reach a home, so groceries, as well as other merchandise, have to be carried from the street. Children often delighted in annoying neighbors by dropping rocks on their roofs. The practice is still around, so the rumors go.

Castle Rock, c. 1932

*C*omposed of Bisbee limestone, Castle Rock is in its way a monument to the mining industry. The first copper and silver ore samples were discovered here by Dunn and Rucker. The spring that led these men here still flows in the basement of the Inn at Castle Rock. Once homes to single miners, several boarding houses across from Castle Rock have been restored as bed and breakfasts for visitors.

Main Street and Chihuahua Hill, c. 1938

$\mathcal{L}$ooking down Main Street in the '30s, you can see what a successful little city Bisbee became. Car dealerships, the mercantile in its temporary headquarters, and a plethora of other stores attest to the wealth generated in Bisbee's mines. Now a tourist mecca, the stores feature metal sculptures, jewelry, antiques, restaurants, and rocks and minerals of the area.

The Top Café, c. 1947

*O*n the top of the divide on the old road to Tombstone, the Top Café did business for many years. It was a place to "get away," though only three miles from downtown. It now serves as a private residence in a lovely site.

Pythian Castle,
c. 1957

The Pythian Castle, built in 1905, was home to the Pythian Lodge, one of Bisbee's many fraternal organizations. The city so enjoyed the clock tower that the job of clock winder became a city position. The building was converted to apartments after a restoration in 1980. The tower is located on OK Street, a narrow two-way street up the side of Brewery Gulch. Young Blood Hill, an inexperienced driver's challenge, leads off OK Street at a forty-five-degree slope to a ninety-degree turn and on to the road at the bottom of Brewery Gulch.

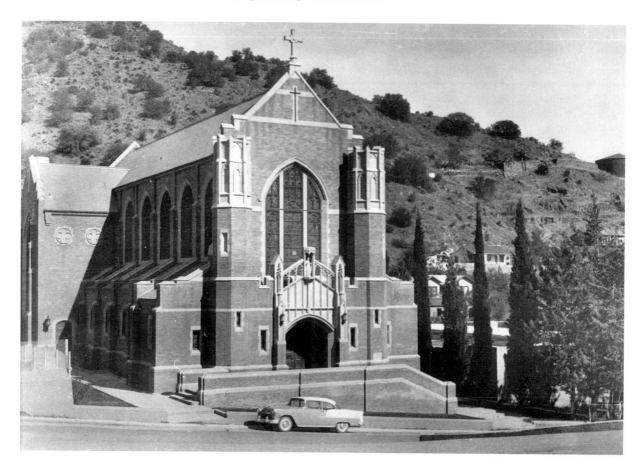

St. Patrick's Church, c. 1957

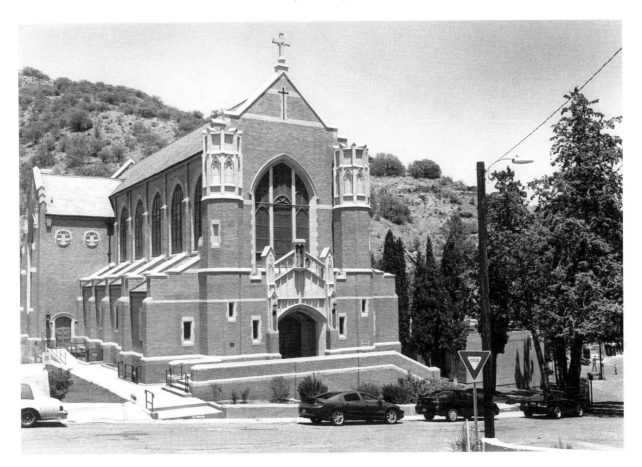

*O*n land donated by Mr. Higgins, an early mine owner, St. Patrick's was built by the Catholic congregation in 1916. Restored recently, the building has a most elegant group of stained glass windows. The church still functions as the largest Catholic Church in the area. A parochial school was housed in adjacent buildings for some forty years.

Main Street, c. 1957

*M*ain Street, also known as Tombstone Canyon, was full of stores meeting the residents' daily needs. Woolworth's, Penney's, several drugstores, jewelry stores, men's haberdasheries, ladies fine wear, as well as the *Bisbee Daily Review* offices, and several restaurants served the public. Wallace Pool Hall, a place where young men learned to play pool and old men suckered visitors into domino games, was a fixture for many years. Now several art galleries and tourist shops line the street. Note that the buildings are the same, but with a new use for the old storefronts.

*B*oyd Nicholl has lived in Bisbee for the last twenty-five years, never having gotten very far from his home town of Tucson. He and his wife raised their daughter in Bisbee and "have prospered, not exactly in the financial sense but in many other ways," he said. They own an 1890s adobe house with a wonderful large yard on the hillside of Moon Canyon. Even the address is rare.

His work has focused on photographs, and, paraphrasing Sammy Sosa's comment about baseball, Boyd claims, "Photography has been very, very good to me." He has taught and worked in photography his entire adult life. His current position as photography and history curator at the Bisbee Mining & Historical museum has been the most satisfying job he has held, combining the two passions of his career.

The photographer used a 35mm Nikon for the "now" photos.

Thank you to the Bisbee Mining & Historical Museum for the use of the historical, or "then," photographs that appear on the left pages of this book.

To purchase *Bisbee, Arizona, Then and Now*
visit the
Bisbee Mining & Historical Museum
5 Copper Queen Plaza, Bisbee, Arizona

or contact
Cowboy Miner Productions at (602) 569-6063
or
visit our website www.CowboyMiner.com.